Another Perfect Day!
Every Day is Dad's Day

Story by Andrew S. Taylor
Illustrations by James G. Martin

An Imprint for GracePoint Publishing
(www.GracePointPublishing.com)

GracePoint Matrix, LLC
624 S. Cascade Ave, Suite 201
Colorado Springs, CO 80903
www.GracePointMatrix.com Email: Admin@GracePointMatrix.com
SAN # 991-6032

A Library of Congress Control Number has been requested and is pending.
ISBN: 978-1-961347-73-1
ISBN: 978-1-961347-74-8

Books may be purchased for educational, business, or sales promotional use.
For bulk order requests and price schedule contact:
Orders@GracePointPublishing.com

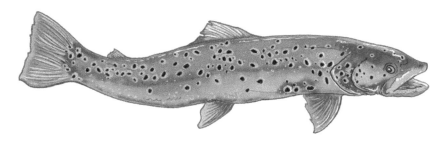

For: George Rosenwald, Steve Hathaway & Cristopher Taylor!

It's thirty years later and its morning in Michigan.
The sun is shining down the street.

The son is watching out the window.

The father, my Dad, has been up for over an hour.

He's got all the gear in the rear of the car and everything is in its proper place.
We're road trip ready. Part one of day one is done. WE'RE GOING FISHING!
It's another perfect pre-day, happily happening.

The driving distance's degree of difficulty is soley dependent on the diversity of the Midwestern weather.

Some years, it's drippy and dreary with little light and lingering, late, no-longer-April showers.

Some years, it's serene and springy with soothing sunshine and sweet smelling Mayflowers.

Today, the travel time is lovely, for as always, inside the car it's completely cool and comfortable. It's early afternoon when we WOW-fully arrive at Grayling, Michigan's Gate's Motel.

It's a wonderful, world-famous full-service fly shop, a highly-regarded all-star restaurant, and an auto-easily-accessible long line of sixteen simple, rustic, redwood, quaintly comfortable, restfully ready, respectable rooms. And, it's all amazingly, appropriately, pleasantly placed along the beautiful banks of the Au Sable River. Ah heaven!

We receive a warm welcome, and check in as easy as walking in the fly shop, smiling, and saying, "Howdy!" We park, unpack, and get our room ready for tomorrow morning's early rising routines. Then, part two of day one beautifully begins, in the best of all possible backyards… it's a picture-perfect rolling river complete with tall trees, green grass, fragrant flowers, and active animals, all in astonishing abundance, all along both banks. We walk down towards a small wooden dock, and we select a sweet swing, serene sitting spot. The rest of the afternoon is spent sipping spirits and delicious drinks, walking, and wonderfully watching the water.

Part three and four of day one is us eating a dectably delicious dinner, retiring to our room, reading and writing in our respective books, and resting 'til tomorrow. Day one is done.
It's another perfect pre-day, happily had.

Part one of day two starts. Sunrise and son-rise are early. As always, it is as it is, even earlier for my Dad. Breakfast begins with coffee, orange juice, and milk and ends with all the expectable, enjoyable, eat-ables.

PICTURE PERFECT PLATES:

COFFEE

ORANGE JUICE

MILK

EGGS: SCRAMBLIED & OVER EASY

HAM & BACON TOAST

French Toast

OATMEAL

PANCAKES

Then it's back to our room, get in gear, and aptly appear back in the parking lot, enthusiastic and early. Our great guide is perfectly punctual.
My dear ole' Dad is delighted. Part two of day two is about to begin.

Everything and everyone is belted in the truck and on the boat.
Then it's a quick-draw drive to the river.
It's another perfect day, happily happening.

Today, launch time is ten-ish.
Dad says, "When you're fishing, nothing is an exact science."
I say, "Yes. That's totally true. And a good thing too."
Dad simply smiles. We're in absolute agreement, and it's time to go with the flow.

At first we free-float and fish on the fly. I stand in front, Dad sits in the middle,
and our great guide steers from the rear. We're a trifective, terrific team.
We fish for fun and photo-ops. It's all catch, click, and release for us.

And as morning moves to afternoon, I am reminded of a favorite *The Hitchhiker's Guide to the Galaxy* quote, "Time is an illusion. Lunchtime doubly so!"

When the fish are not earnestly eating our man-made morsels, we eagerly eat our hand-made meals. Scrumptious sandwiches, bratwurst and buns, char-grilled chicken, or sizzling steaks are all served with potatoes or fruit salad, chips, and chocolate chip cookies, or chewy-fudgy, no-nut brownies. And all throughout the day, there's sweet tea, bottled water, and iced or hot coffee from a thermos. It's a yummy in your tummy, plethora of plenty.

Part two of day two casually continues.

As we slowly slip down the steady, calm currents of the rolling river, rods and reels softly sing. False flies fall on all our aptly-aimed-for hot spots, and anxious anticipation accompanies every free-floating, hopeful hook.

The royal river is full of fantastic fish. And if the fishing fates favor us, so will our soon-to-be softly spoken, soul-smiling, super-sized stories.

Part two of day two easily ends sometime between four-ish and five-ish. Last casts are heroically thrown to last spots just to see if one more fabulous fish can be caught, pictured, and thus so honorably owned.

Take out is quickly taken care of, our drive back is quietly brief, and day three's oh-so-sweet same schedule is simply set.

Day two is done after we eat another delectably delicious dinner complete with hot, creamy soups, simple salads, some best burgers or select specials, and a few fresh-each-day, newly-made, delicious desserts.

It was another pefect day, happily had.

Day four, we diligently drive home sweet home.

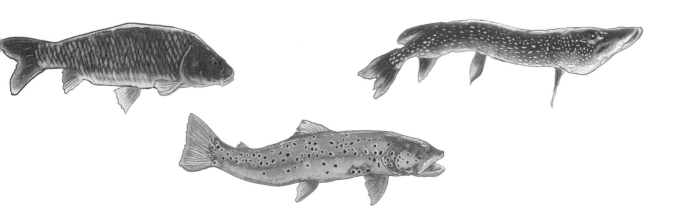

Thanks for all these newly made,
magical memories, Dad!

Love, Andrew! A+ 😊

With an abundance of appreciation for:

Everyone at Gates Lodge, Au Sable River-Grayling, MI,
Josh Greenberg & All Their Families!
AND... Josh Nethers & All His Family!

THANKS FOR ALL THE
FANTASTIC FISHING!

TaylorEDTime.com A+

About the Author

Andrew S. Taylor holds two BSED degrees in Pre-K-12, Elementary and Secondary Education Theater/Speech. As a self-employed entrepreneur, he is a teenage through adult Life Enrichment Teacher, Creativity Workshop Facilitator, Special Event Public Speaker, and Personal/Professional Life Coach/Consultant. He is equally proficient with individuals, couples, and large-scale groups. At Interlochen National Arts Camp, he was Divisional Honor Camper ('87 H.S.B. Theater Major) and Honor Cabin Counselor ('05 & '07). He was his university's Muppet Mascot, The OU Bobcat, a Pre-K-12 Child Care Teacher/Program Director for eight years, and also The Children's Department Supervisor & Storytime Reader, at a super-sized Barnes & Noble, for four years.

When not every day, enthusiastically engaged in creative writing, his hobbies include collating his colossal collection of Movies & TV Shows (2,800+DISKS!), making beaded jewelry (pins, necklaces, and friendship bracelets), and acting in Community Theater. Mr. Taylor lives in Ann Arbor, MI, and can be contacted at www.TaylorEDTime.com.

About the Illustrator

James G. Martin is a professional artist and illustrator with over thirty years of experience in product design for McDonald's Happy Meal toys, retail toys and holiday giftware. He has enjoyed working on the world's most popular licenses from Walt Disney Pictures, Pixar, DreamWorks, and Cartoon Network to name a few!

He resides in Kansas City, MO. with his family and their two dogs, Walter and Grubby. You can see more of his art at www.mrmartinart.com.

OTHER BOOKS BY ANDREW S. TAYLOR

BIRDS!

The Phenomenal Phoenix!

Something Small

A Cloud & The Eye of the Beholder

Mommy, Am I BEAUTIFUL?

LULLABY-ed Child

Sitting in the Lap of Love!

Every Day is Mother's Day: Sitting in the Sunroom of My Sweetest Sanctuary

A Perfect Day!

TaylorED Time: How to Dramatically Build Your Character
& Live the Life FANTASTIC!

TaylorED Time Workbook: How to Be the Captain
of Your Character's Creation